Getting Ready
to
Cook

ISBN 0-918831-30-X

U.S. Edition Copyright © 1985 by Gareth Stevens, Inc.

First published in South Africa by Daan Retief Publishers
Copyright © 1983.

U.S. Editor: Joseph F. Westphal
Cover Illustrations: Renée Graef
Typeset by Colony Pre-Press • Milwaukee, WI 53208 USA

Getting Ready to Cook

S.J.A. de Villiers
and
Eunice van der Berg

Illustrated By
Marita Johnson

Gareth Stevens — Milwaukee

First Cookbook Library

Getting Ready To Cook
Drinks and Desserts
One Dish Meals
Vegetables and Salads
Breads and Biscuits
Cookies, Cakes and Candies

These books will show you how easy it is to cook and what fun it is, too.

Everything you have to do is clearly illustrated and the methods you will learn are the same as those used in advanced cookbooks. Once you learn these methods you will be able to follow recipes you find in any cookbook.

In this book you will learn how to make a tasty and nutritious meal using just one dish. Choose any one of these recipes to make a meal for your family.

If you are concerned about salt, sugar and fats in your diet, you may reduce the amount called for or substitute other ingredients in many of the recipes. Ask an adult for suggestions.

CONTENTS

Black arrows ➡ in some recipes are
reminders to ask a grown-up to help
you.

Getting Ready

1. Ask your parents, or anyone else who can help, to read the recipe with you and show you how to use the kitchen equipment.

2. Wash your hands thoroughly before you start working. Put on an apron to protect your clothes. If you have long hair, tie it back.

3. Set out everything that you need for the recipe before you start working. It is also a good idea to measure dry ingredients beforehand.

Remember

1. Use potholders or oven mitts to handle pots, pans, and anything hot from the stove so that you do not burn your fingers.

➡ Black arrows in some recipes are reminders to ask a grownup to help you.

2. Turn the handles of saucepans on the stove so that they don't get in your way.

3. Stir hot mixtures with a wooden spoon. A metal spoon might burn your fingers.

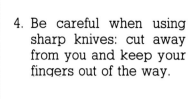

4. Be careful when using sharp knives: cut away from you and keep your fingers out of the way.

When grating cheese or carrots, make sure that your fingers do not touch the grater. When using electric equipment, get an adult to help you.

5. Spilled food on the floor might cause an accident. Mop up spills immediately with a sponge or paper towel.

Afterwards

1. Wash up when you have finished. Utensils used for eggs should first be soaked in cold water. Washing up will then be easier.

2. Put everything you have used back where it belongs. Leave the kitchen tidy so that you will be allowed to work there again.

Facts About Foods

Eating is fun, but you also have to eat certain foods to grow and to keep healthy.

Select food from each of the following groups every day.

1. **Meat, Fish, Poultry, Eggs, Milk, Cheese, Nuts, Dry Beans,** and **Peanut Butter.**

   This group contains proteins and minerals which make you grow.

2. **Breads, Cereals, Noodles,** and **Rice.**

   This group contains carbohydrates which provide energy.

3. Fruit and Vegetables

Green vegetables, like green beans, and yellow vegetables, like carrots, contain vitamins and minerals which keep you healthy. Oranges and grapefruits contain vitamin C which helps prevent colds. Fresh fruits and vegetables are more nutritious than canned or frozen fruits and vegetables.

4. Sugar, Butter, Cream, and Margarine

These add flavor to foods and provide energy; however, you will put on weight if you eat too much of these.

Measuring Correctly

Before you start cooking, you must learn to measure ingredients correctly.

The three main systems of measuring are American Standard, Imperial, and Metric. American Standard and Imperial are similar, but Metric is quite different.

Weight is measured in ounces in American Standard and in grams in Metric. Usually the weight of a product can be found on the package. Volume: the contents of a cup are measured in ounces in American Standard and in milliliters ("ml" for short) in Metric. Measuring spoons and measuring cups are used for this purpose.

American Standard measuring spoons come in four sizes: ¼ teaspoon, ½ teaspoon, 1 teaspoon, and 1 tablespoon. Use these spoons to measure dry ingredients and liquids. (Metric countries measure in ml as shown in the illustrations.)

Lengths and widths of pans and baking sheets are measured in inches or centimeters ("cm" for short). Use a measuring tape or ruler to do this.

Use a glass or plastic measuring cup to measure liquids like milk, water, or oil. Put the cup on the table, and, with your eyes level with the mark on the cup, make sure you have the right amount.

A set of measuring cups is made up of four sizes: ¼ cup, ⅓ cup, ½ cup and 1 cup. Use the size you need to measure dry ingredients like sugar and flour. Spoon the sugar or flour into the clean cup and level off the top with a knife. Do not press the ingredients into the cup.

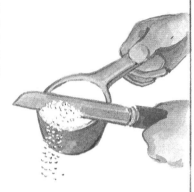

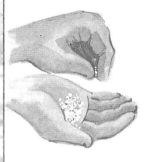

A pinch of salt is the amount you can hold between two fingers.

The two measuring spoons you will use most often are the tablespoon and the teaspoon.

Butter and margarine are sometimes sold in one pound blocks. Cut it through the middle to get two ½ pound blocks. Divide ½ pound and get two ¼ pound blocks (8 ounces).

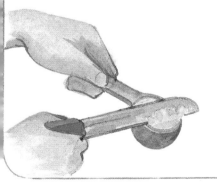

To measure one tablespoon butter, press butter firmly into a tablespoon, leveling it off with a knife.

Converting Oven Temperatures and Measurements

Ovens and oven temperatures

Oven temperature is regulated by a thermometer in the oven. When an oven is switched on to preheat, a tiny light goes on. As soon as the oven reaches the desired temperature, the light goes out. For gas or other ovens without a light indicator, preheat the oven for 10 to 15 minutes. You can then place your dish in the oven. The chart below lists the conversions from Farenheit to Celsius.

Very cool	= 100° C	= 250° F
Cool	= 140° C	= 300° F
Medium	= 180° C	= 350° F
Medium hot	= 190° C	= 375° F
Hot	= 200° C	= 400° F
Very hot	= 230° C	= 450° F

Converting measurements from American Standard to Metric

The measurements given in this cookbook are the ones used in the United States, called American Standard measurements. Other countries may use the metric system for measurement. This chart will show you the equivalent metric measurements for the Standard measurements used in this cookbook.

1 teaspoon	=	5 Milliliters
1 tablespoon	=	15 Milliliters

¼ cup	=	62.5 Milliliters
⅓ cup	=	85 Milliliters
½ cup	=	125 Milliliters
1 cup	=	250 Milliliters

Kitchen Equipment

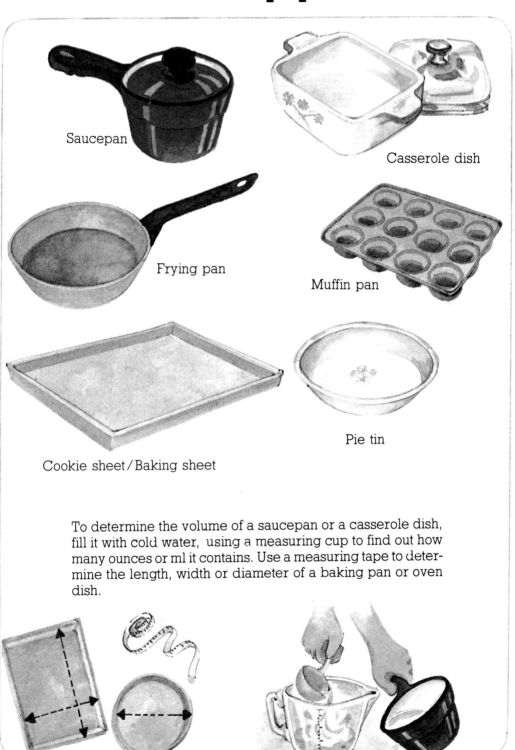

Saucepan

Casserole dish

Frying pan

Muffin pan

Cookie sheet / Baking sheet

Pie tin

To determine the volume of a saucepan or a casserole dish, fill it with cold water, using a measuring cup to find out how many ounces or ml it contains. Use a measuring tape to determine the length, width or diameter of a baking pan or oven dish.

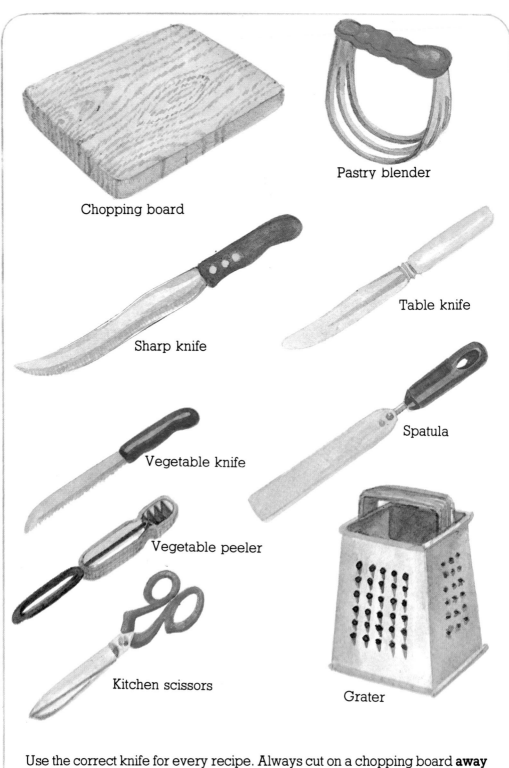

Chopping board

Pastry blender

Sharp knife

Table knife

Vegetable knife

Spatula

Vegetable peeler

Kitchen scissors

Grater

Use the correct knife for every recipe. Always cut on a chopping board **away from yourself.**

Wooden spoon

Plastic scraper

Vegetable brush

Kitchen tongs

Sieve

Colander

Pastry brush

Pancake turner

Electric
hand mixer

Cooling rack

Food processor

Egg beater

Words To Know

➡ Bake: cook in the oven.

Batter: a runny mixture of flour, liquid and other ingredients. It is possible to pour it from one container to another as one does with pancake batter or cake batter.

➡ Boil: heat in a liquid until air bubbles rise rapidly from the bottom of the pan and break on the surface.

Break an egg: crack the egg shell on the side of a bowl. Place both your thumbs on the crack and break open the egg so that its contents drop into a bowl. Throw away the egg shell.

➡ Chop: use a sharp knife to cut onions, green peppers, parsley, and nuts, etc., into small pieces. Use rapid up and down movements, holding the tip of the chopping knife on the board with one hand and the handle with the other. A food processor chops much faster.

Cream: use the back of a wooden spoon to rub butter or margarine against the sides of a mixing bowl until it looks creamy. Add sugar gradually.

Cut in: blend the butter or margarine with flour using a table knife or pastry blender. The mixture must be fine and look like soft bread crumbs.

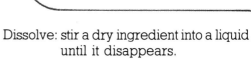

Dissolve: stir a dry ingredient into a liquid until it disappears.

Dough: a stiff mixture of flour, liquid and other ingredients. It may be lumpy, or kneaded to form one smooth piece of dough (such as sugar dough).

Drain: to separate liquids from solids. Pour the mixture into a sieve or colander resting on a mixing bowl.

Flake: use two forks to break boiled fish into small pieces.

Fold in: carefully turn the mixture over using a metal spoon. The spoon should touch the mixing bowl with every turn. This method of mixing is the best way to retain most of the air whisked into one of your ingredients like egg whites.

➡ Fry: cook in oil or butter in a pan.

Jelling: the process in which a liquid changes to form a solid, as in the case of gelatin.

Grate: rub cheese or vegetables against the grid of a grater to break it into regular, fine pieces.

Grease: spread a little margarine or oil on a baking pan or oven dish before baking food on it. Use a piece of wax paper to spread the oil, butter, or margarine.

Knead: mix dough by pressing and turning it with your hands until it becomes smooth and elastic.

➡ Melt: heat solids like butter until they form liquids.

Mix: combine ingredients until they are evenly blended.

Rub in: blend butter or margarine with flour by rubbing it with your finger tips. You may grate hard (cold) butter or margarine first. Work quickly so the heat from your fingers does not melt the butter.

Separate an egg: break open an egg shell carefully. Keep the yolk in one half of the shell while the white runs into one bowl. Drop the yolk into another bowl.

Shred: use a pair of scissors to cut off tiny pieces of parsley leaves. Hold a small bunch of parsley tightly in one hand while cutting carefully with the other.

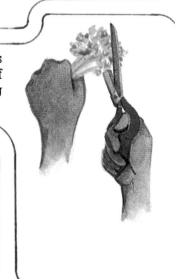

➡ Simmer: allow a liquid mixture to cook over a low heat (for a specific time). Do not stir.

➡ Stew: cook food like fruit or tough meat over low heat in a little water. Cook slowly until soft or tender.

➡ Stir: move a spoon in circles through a mixture in a saucepan or a mixing bowl to mix ingredients and to prevent burning. The spoon should touch the bottom of the saucepan or bowl.

➡ Stir-fry: stir chopped or shredded vegetables in a little hot margarine or oil in a frying pan until evenly done. Use a wooden spoon and switch on the burner to medium heat.

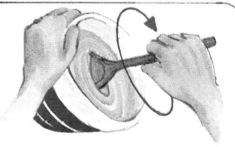

Whip: use a wooden spoon in a rapid up and down movement around the inside of a mixing bowl to get air into the mixture.

Whisk: use an egg beater to mix liquids fast or to whisk a lot of tiny air bubbles into a food like gelatin or egg whites.

Helpful Hints For Cooking

➡ To peel tomatoes: Put them in a bowl and cover with boiling water. Leave for two minutes. Lift them out with a slotted spoon and place them in a bowl filled with cold water. The skins will come off easily. Always do this when using tomatoes in a hot dish.

Cold drinks stay fizzy longer if they are served ice cold.

Peeled bananas, avocados and apples turn brown when exposed to air. Squeeze lemon juice over them to prevent discoloration and keep them looking fresh.

Store lettuce and vegetables in air-tight containers or plastic bags in the refrigerator and they will stay fresh longer.

Gelatin sets best in the refrigerator. It will not set faster in a freezer.

Sprinkle a little powdered sugar over custard so that a skin does not form on top. Or place round pieces of wax paper on top.

Packing sandwiches for a bag lunch: when the sandwiches are wrapped tightly in plastic and chilled well in the refrigerator before packing, they will stay fresh longer.

Store cakes and cookies in air-tight containers. Cakes will stay soft and fresh and cookies will remain crisp. (Always handle cookies carefully to prevent them from breaking or crumbling).

An attractive box of cookies tied with ribbon makes a lovely present. Line the box with wax paper and place the paper between rows or layers of cookies. Pack the layers tightly together so that the cookies will not move around and crumble.

Chocolate Milk Shake

(1 serving)

Take Out:

1 shaker with a tight lid
1 soup spoon
measuring cups
measuring spoons
1 large glass

What You'll Need

Vanilla or chocolate ice cream
2 tablespoons chocolate syrup
½ cup cold milk

1. Spoon five or six spoons ice cream into the shaker. Add the chocolate syrup and milk. Stir.

2. Put the lid on the shaker and shake well until blended. You can use a blender instead.

3. Pour into the glass and serve immediately.

Tossed Green Salad

(4 servings)

Take Out:

salad bowl
vegetable peeler
chopping board
vegetable knife

measuring cups
measuring spoons
mixing bowl
salad servers

What You'll Need

6 crisp lettuce leaves
½ small cucumber
2 tomatoes
4 green onions

pinch of salt
½ ripe avocado
¼ cup salad dressing

1. Wash and dry the lettuce leaves and break them into small pieces in the salad bowl.

➡ 2. Peel the cucumber and cut it into cubes. Spread it over the lettuce.

➡ 3. Wash and cut the tomatoes into wedges. Arrange them over the cucumber.

4. Wash the onions under cold, running water. Pull off the thin outer skin and cut off the roots and some of the green leaves.

➡ 5. Cut the onions into small rings and sprinkle over the tomato in the salad bowl.

➡ 6. Cut the avocado lengthwise into two halves and remove the pit. Peel one half carefully.

➡ 7. Dice this half and arrange over the other layers. Ripe avocado bruises easily, so be careful!

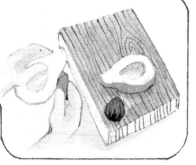

8. Shake the bottle of dressing and pour ¼ cup over the salad just before serving.

9. Toss the salad and dressing lightly using the salad servers. Move the salad around until all the ingredients are evenly coated with the dressing.

Tuna Casserole
(4 servings)

Take Out:

can opener
casserole dish (1 quart)
mixing bowl
egg beater
spoon

fork
plastic bag
rolling pin
measuring cups
oven mitts

What You'll Need

1 can cream of chicken soup (10 ¾ ounces)
1 egg
⅔ cup milk
1 can tuna (6-¾ ounce)
1 cup cooked or canned green peas
2 cups potato chips

➡ 1. Preheat the oven to 350°.

➡ 2. Open the can of soup and pour the contents into the casserole.

3. Beat the egg and milk together in the mixing bowl. Mix in the casserole using a fork.

4. Put the potato chips in a plastic bag but do not tie the bag. Crush them with the rolling pin. Add half of the crushed chips to the soup mixture.

5. Flake the tuna with a fork and add to the soup mixture.

6. Lastly, stir in the peas and level the top with the fork. Sprinkle the remaining crushed chips on top.

➡ 7. Bake for 30 minutes. Use oven mitts to remove the casserole from the oven. Turn off the oven heat.

8. Serve with a mixed green salad.

Crispies

(makes about 24 squares)

Take Out:

flat dish or pan
measuring cups
measuring spoons
mixing bowl

wooden spoon
double boiler
spatula
serving dish

What You'll Need:

5 cups crisp rice cereal
½ cup chopped pecans
¼ cup butter or margarine

1 10 ounce package
marshmallows
⅓ teaspoon vanilla extract

1. Grease the flat dish or pan.

2. Measure the cereal and the nuts into the mixing bowl.

➡ 3. Pour three cups hot water into the bottom of the double boiler. Put it on the stove and turn on the heat to medium. Leave it to boil.

➡ 4. Measure the butter into the top of the double boiler and put it on the hot water.

➡ 5. Add the marshmallows to the butter in the top part of the double boiler. Stir until they have melted. Add the vanilla and stir.

➡ 6. Turn off the heat. Pour the hot marshmallow mixture over the cereal in the mixing bowl. Stir until the rice crispies and nuts cling together.

7. Press the mixture into the greased pan with the spatula.

8. Leave it to cool and cut into squares. Use the spatula to lift out the crispies onto the serving dish.

INDEX